FOREST PARK PUBLIC LIBRARY

3 2026 00355

P9-CCJ-628

WITHDRAWN

NOV - - 2015

FOREST PARK PUBLIC LIBRARY
7555 Jackson Blvd.
Forest Park, IL 60130
708-366-7171
www.fppl.org

ARDENNES 1944

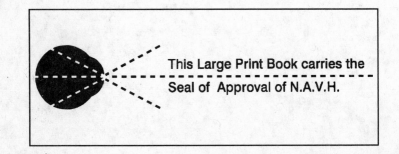

This Large Print Book carries the
Seal of Approval of N.A.V.H.

ARDENNES 1944

THE BATTLE OF THE BULGE

ANTONY BEEVOR

THORNDIKE PRESS
A part of Gale, Cengage Learning

FOREST PARK PUBLIC LIBRARY

NOV   2015

FOREST PARK, IL

GALE
CENGAGE Learning·

Farmington Hills, Mich • San Francisco • New York • Waterville, Maine
Meriden, Conn • Mason, Ohio • Chicago

GALE
CENGAGE Learning®

Copyright © 2015 by Ocito Ltd.
Map illustrations by Jeff Edwards.
Thorndike Press, a part of Gale, Cengage Learning.

ALL RIGHTS RESERVED
Thorndike Press® Large Print Popular and Narrative Nonfiction.
The text of this Large Print edition is unabridged.
Other aspects of the book may vary from the original edition.
Set in 16 pt. Plantin.

LIBRARY OF CONGRESS CATALOGING-IN-PUBLICATION DATA

Names: Beevor, Antony, 1946- author.
Title: Ardennes 1944 : the Battle of the Bulge / by Antony Beevor.
Description: Large print edition. | Waterville, Maine : Thorndike Press, 2015. |
    Series: Thorndike press large print popular and narrative nonfiction Includes
    bibliographical references.
Identifiers: LCCN 2015038737| ISBN 9781410483720 (hardcover) | ISBN
    141048372X (hardcover)
Subjects: LCSH: Ardennes, Battle of the, 1944-1945.
Classification: LCC D756.5.A7 B44 2015 | DDC 940.54/219348—dc23
LC record available at http://lccn.loc.gov/2015038737

Published in 2015 by arrangement with Viking, an imprint of Penguin
Publishing Group, a division of Penguin Random House LLC

Printed in the United States of America
1 2 3 4 5 6 7 19 18 17 16 15

For Adam Beevor

CONTENTS

LIST OF ILLUSTRATIONS

Illustration acknowledgements

The majority of the photographs come from The National Archives in the USA. Other photographs are from: 1, 13, AKG Images; 5, Documentation Française; 11, Tank Museum; 12, Bundesarchiv, Koblenz; 6–7, 18, 20, 25–6, 30–32, 34, 36, 38–9, 41, 46–7, US Army (part of National Archives); 8, 23, 26, 40, Imperial War Museum, London; 10, Heinz Seidler, Bonn Bad Godersberg, reproduced from W. Goolrick and O. Tanner, *The Battle of the Bulge.*

LIST OF MAPS

Key to Military Symbols

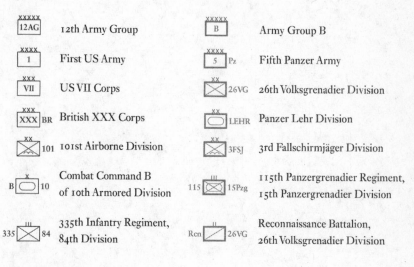

Allied

XXXXX 12AG	12th Army Group
XXXX 1	First US Army
XXX VII	US VII Corps
XXX XXX BR	British XXX Corps
XX 101	101st Airborne Division
B X 10	Combat Command B of 10th Armored Division
335 III 84	335th Infantry Regiment, 84th Division

German

XXXXX B	Army Group B
XXXX 5 Pz	Fifth Panzer Army
XX 26VG	26th Volksgrenadier Division
XX LEHR	Panzer Lehr Division
XX 3FSJ	3rd Fallschirmjäger Division
115 III 15Pzg	115th Panzergrenadier Regiment, 15th Panzergrenadier Division
Rcn II 26VG	Reconnaissance Battalion, 26th Volksgrenadier Division

GLOSSARY

Abatis Barriers across roads and tracks made by cutting down and dropping trees, which were often mined or booby-trapped.

Com Z The Communications Zone commanded by General Lee responsible for all supplies and replacement soldiers.

Counter Intelligence Corps The US Army equivalent of the British Field Security.

CSDIC Combined Services Detailed Interrogation Centre included those holding pens and prison camps, such as Trent Park in England, where the conversation of German prisoners was secretly recorded by mainly German Jewish volunteers.

Dogface US Army slang for an infantryman.

Doughboy A term from the First World War for an ordinary American soldier.

G-2 Senior staff officer or staff for intelligence.

G-3 Senior staff officer or staff for operations.

Jabo German abbreviation for fighter-bomber or *Jagdbomber.*

Kübelwagen The German army's counterpart to the Jeep, it was made by Volkswagen and slightly larger and heavier.

Meat-chopper US Army slang for anti-aircraft half-track mounting quadruple .50 machine guns when used against enemy infantry.

Meuse river The French and English name for the river which German, Dutch and Flemish speakers called the Maas.

Non-battle casualties Include the sick, those suffering from trench foot or frostbite, and neuropsychiatric or combat-fatigue breakdown.

Pozit fuses These 'proximity' fuses for artillery shells, used for the first time in the Ardennes, exploded with devastating effect as air bursts above the enemy's heads.

PX The Post Exchange, which sold items, including cigarettes, to US Army personnel.

Roer river Rur river in German, but here for the sake of clarity given the Flemish/French/English name of Roer even on German territory.

SA Sturmabteilung, the Nazi 'brownshirt' stormtroopers.

Schloss German castle, or large country house.

Screaming meemies The US Army slang for the German six-barrelled Nebelwerfer rocket launcher which made a terrifying sound.

SHAEF Supreme Headquarters Allied Expeditionary Force. General Eisenhower's headquarters based at Versailles commanding the three army groups on the western front.

Trench foot Trench foot was officially called 'immersion foot' in the US Army, but everyone continued to use the First World War term of 'trench foot'. It was a form of foot rot which was due to damp feet, a failure to change to dry socks and a lack of mobility. It could become gangrenous.

Ultra The interception of German signals prepared on Enigma machines which were decoded at Bletchley Park.

Volksgrenadier German infantry divisions reconstituted in the autumn of 1944 with a smaller establishment.

Wehrmachtführungsstab The Wehrmacht operations staff led by Generaloberst Jodl.

Westwall German name for the defence line on the Reich's western border which the Americans and British called the Siegfried Line.

TABLE OF MILITARY RANKS

American	British	German army	Waffen-SS
Private	Private/Trooper	Schütze/Kanonier/Jäger	Schütze
Private First Class		Oberschütze	Oberschütze
	Lance-Corporal	Gefreiter	Sturmmann
Corporal	Corporal	Obergefreiter	Rottenführer
Sergeant	Sergeant	Feldwebel/Wachtmeister	Oberscharführer
Staff Sergeant	Staff/Colour Sergeant	Oberfeldwebel	Hauptscharführer
Technical Sergeant	Regtl Quartermaster Sgt		
Master Sergeant	Coy/Sqn Sergeant Major	Stabsfeldwebel	Sturmscharführer
	Regimental Sergeant Major		
2nd Lieutenant	2nd Lieutenant	Leutnant	Untersturmführer
Lieutenant	Lieutenant	Oberleutnant	Obersturmführer
Captain	Captain	Hauptmann/Rittmeister	Hauptsturmführer
Major	Major	Major	Sturmbannführer
Lieutenant Colonel	Lieutenant Colonel	Oberstleutnant	Obersturmbannführer
Colonel	Colonel	Oberst	Standartenführer
Brigadier General	Brigadier *	Generalmajor	Oberführer
			Brigadeführer
Major General	Major General **	Generalleutnant	Gruppenführer

Lieutenant General	Lieutenant General	***	General der Infanterie/ Artillerie/Panzertruppe	Obergruppenführer/ General der Waffen-SS
General	General	****	Generaloberst	Obergruppenführer
General of the Army	Field Marshal	*****	Generalfeldmarschall	

This can only be an approximate guide to equivalent ranks since each army has its own variations. Some ranks have been omitted in the interests of simplicity. In the British and US armies the following ranks command the following sub-units (below a battalion), units (battalion or regiment) and formations (brigade, division or corps).

Rank	British and Canadian army	US Army	Approx. number of men at full strength
Corporal	Section	Squad	8
2nd/Lieutenant	Platoon	Platoon	30
Captain/Major	Company	Company	120
Lieutenant Colonel	Battalion or Armoured Regiment	Battalion	700
Colonel		Regiment	2,400
Brigadier	Brigade	Combat command	2,400
Major General	Division	Division	10,000
Lieutenant General	Corps	Corps	30,000–40,000
General	Army	Army	70,000–150,000
Field Marshal/ General of the Army	Army Group	Army Group	200,000–350,000

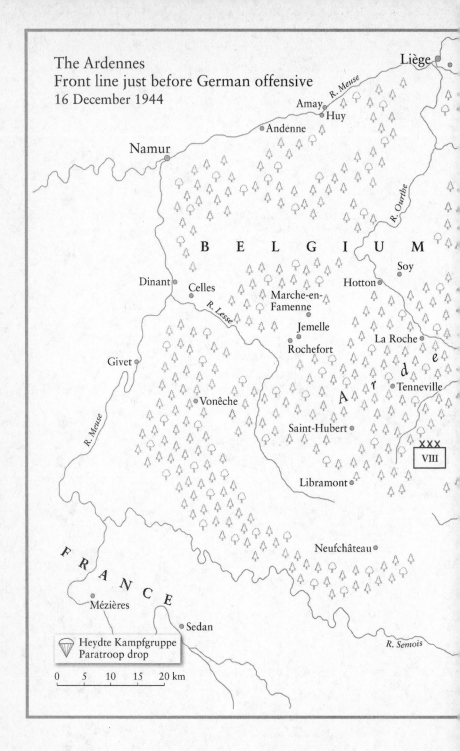

The Ardennes
Front line just before German offensive
16 December 1944

Liège

R. Meuse

Amay
Huy

Andenne

Namur

R. Ourthe

B E L G I U M

Soy

Dinant

Celles

Marche-en-Famenne

Hotton

Jemelle

Rochefort

La Roche

Givet

Saint-Hubert

Vonêche

A r d e

Tenneville

XXX
VIII

Libramont

R. Lesse

R. Meuse

Neufchâteau

F R A N C E

Mézières

Sedan

R. Semois

Heydte Kampfgruppe
Paratroop drop

0   5   10   15   20 km

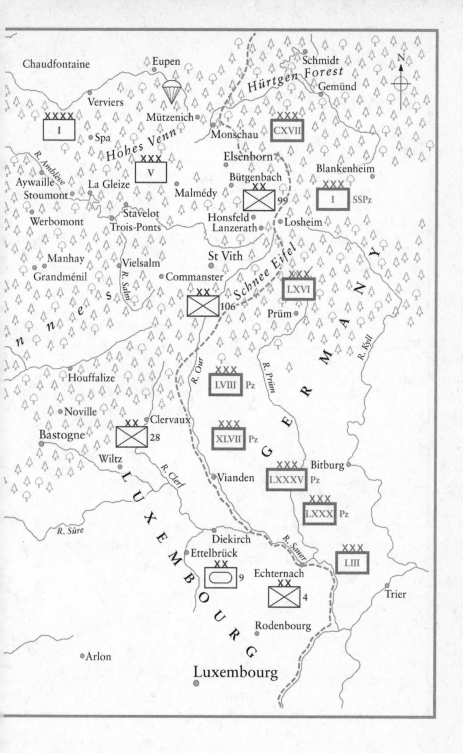

The Ardennes
Furthest point of German advance
25 December 1944

Liège

R. Meuse

Amay
Huy
Andenne

Namur

R. Ourthe

B E L G I U M

Soy

Dinant
Celles
Hotton

R. Lesse

Marche-en-
Famenne

Jemelle

La Roche

Rochefort

Givet

Tenneville

Vonêche

Saint-Hubert

R. Meuse

Libramont

Neufchâteau

F R A N C E

Mézières

Sedan

R. Semois

0   5   10   15   20 km

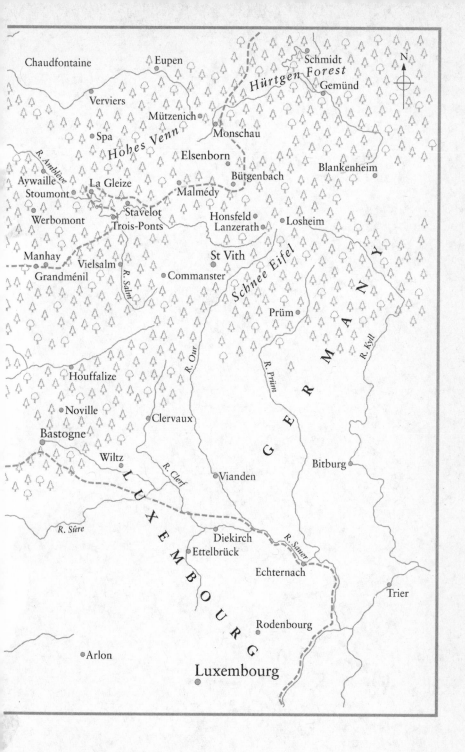

1
VICTORY FEVER

Early on 27 August 1944, General Dwight
D. Eisenhower left Chartres to see the newly
liberated Paris. 'It's Sunday,' the Supreme Allied Commander told General Omar Brad-
'ey, whom he took with him. 'Everyone will
be sleeping late. We can do it without any
fuss.' Yet the two generals were hardly incon-
spicuous as they bowled along towards the
French capital on their supposedly 'informal
visit'. The Supreme Commander's olive-drab
Cadillac was escorted by two armoured cars,
and a Jeep with a brigadier general leading
the way.

When they reached the Porte d'Orléans, an
even larger escort from the 38th Cavalry
Reconnaissance Squadron awaited in review
order under the orders of Major General Gerow. Leonard Gerow, an old friend of Eisenhower, still seethed with resentment because
General Philippe Leclerc of the French 2nd
Armoured Division had consistently disobeyed all his orders during the advance on

Paris. The day before, Gerow, who considered himself the military governor of Paris, had forbidden Leclerc and his division to take part in General de Gaulle's procession from the Arc de Triomphe to Notre-Dame. He had told him instead to 'continue on present mission of clearing Paris and environs of enemy'. Leclerc had ignored Gerow throughout the liberation of the capital, but that morning he had sent part of his division north out of the city against German positions around Saint-Denis.

The streets of Paris were empty because the retreating Germans had seized almost every vehicle that could move. Even the Métro was unpredictable because of the feeble power supply; in fact the so-called 'City of Light' was reduced to candles bought on the black market. Its beautiful buildings looked faded and tired, although they were mercifully intact. Hitler's order to reduce it to 'a field of rubble' had not been followed. In the immediate aftermath of joy, groups in the street still cheered every time they caught sight of an American soldier or vehicle. Yet it would not be long before the Parisians started muttering 'Pire que les boches' — 'Worse than the Boches'.

Despite Eisenhower's remark about going to Paris 'without any fuss', their visit had a definite purpose. They went to meet General Charles de Gaulle, the leader of the French provisional government which President Roosevelt refused to recognize. Eisenhower, a pragmatist, was prepared to ignore his President's firm instruction that United States forces in France were not there to install General de Gaulle in power. The Supreme Commander needed stability behind his front lines, and since de Gaulle was the only man likely to provide it, he was willing to support him.

Neither de Gaulle nor Eisenhower wanted the dangerous chaos of liberation to get out of hand, especially at a time of frenzied rumours, sudden panics, conspiracy theories and the ugly denunciations of alleged collaborators. Together with a comrade, the writer J. D. Salinger, a Counter Intelligence Corps staff sergeant with the 4th Infantry Division, had arrested a suspect in an action close to the Hôtel de Ville, only for the crowd to drag him away and beat him to death in front of their eyes. De Gaulle's triumphal procession the day before from the Arc de Triomphe to Notre-Dame had ended in wild fusillades within the cathedral itself. This incident convinced de Gaulle that he must disarm the Resistance and conscript its members into a regular French army. A request for 15,000 uniforms was passed that very afternoon to SHAEF — the Supreme

Headquarters Allied Expeditionary Force.*
Unfortunately, there were not enough small
sizes because the average French male was
distinctly shorter than his American contem-
porary.

De Gaulle's meeting with the two American
generals took place in the ministry of war in
the rue Saint-Dominique. This was where his
short-lived ministerial career had begun in
the tragic summer of 1940, and he had
returned there to emphasize the impression
of continuity. His formula for erasing the
shame of the Vichy regime was a majestically
simple one: 'The Republic has never ceased
to exist.' De Gaulle wanted Eisenhower to
keep Leclerc's division in Paris to ensure law
and order, but since some of Leclerc's units
had now started to move out, he suggested
that perhaps the Americans could impress
the population with 'a show of force' to re-
assure them that the Germans would not be
coming back. Why not march a whole division or even two through Paris on its way to
the front? Eisenhower, thinking it slightly
ironic that de Gaulle should be asking for
American troops 'to establish his position
firmly', turned to Bradley and asked what he
thought. Bradley said that it would be per-
fectly possible to arrange within the next
couple of days. So Eisenhower invited de

* See Glossary.

Gaulle to take the salute, accompanied by General Bradley. He himself would stay away.

On their return to Chartres, Eisenhower invited General Sir Bernard Montgomery to join de Gaulle and Bradley for the parade, but he refused to come to Paris. Such a small but pertinent detail did not deter certain British newspapers from accusing the Americans of trying to hog all the glory for themselves. Inter-Allied relations were to be severely damaged by the compulsion in Fleet Street to see almost every decision by SHAEF as a slight to Montgomery and thus the British. This reflected the more widespread resentment that Britain was being sidelined. The Americans were now running the show and would claim the victory for themselves. Eisenhower's British deputy, Air Chief Marshal Sir Arthur Tedder, was alarmed by the prejudice of the English press: 'From what I heard at SHAEF, I could not help fearing that this process was sowing the seeds of a grave split between the Allies.'

The following evening the 28th Infantry Division, under its commander, Major General Norman D. Cota, moved from Versailles towards Paris in heavy rain. 'Dutch' Cota, who had shown extraordinary bravery and leadership on Omaha beach, had taken over command less than two weeks before, after a German sniper had killed his predecessor. The fighting in the heavy hedgerow country of Normandy had been slow and deadly during June and July, but the breakout led by General George S. Patton's Third Army at the beginning of August had produced a surge of optimism during the charge to the River Seine and Paris itself.

Showers had been set up for Cota's men in the Bois de Boulogne so that they could scrub themselves before the parade. The next morning, 29 August, the division set off up the Avenue Foch to the Arc de Triomphe, and then down the long vista of the Champs-Elysées. Helmeted infantry, with rifles slung and bayonets fixed, marched in full battle order. The mass of olive-drab, rank after rank twenty-four men abreast, stretched right across the broad avenue. Each man on his shoulder wore the divisional badge, the red 'Keystone' symbol of Pennsylvania, which the Germans had dubbed the 'bloody bucket' from its shape.

The French were amazed, both by the informality of American uniforms and by their seemingly limitless quantities of machinery. 'Une armée de mécanos,' the diarist Jean Galtier-Boissière remarked. On the Champs-Elysées that morning, the French crowds could not believe that a single infantry division could have so many vehicles: countless Jeeps, some with .50 machine guns mounted behind; scout-cars; the artillery, with their 155mm 'Long Tom' howitzers towed by tracked prime-movers; engineers; service units with small trucks and ten-tonners; M-4 Sherman tanks, and tank destroyers. This display made the Wehrmacht, the apparently invincible conqueror of France in 1940, appear bizarrely old-fashioned with its horse-drawn transport.

The saluting dais was on the Place de la Concorde. Army engineers had created it out of assault boats turned upside down and concealed by a long *tricolore* valance, while numerous Stars and Stripes fluttered in the breeze. In front the fifty-six-piece band, which had led the parade, played the division's march, 'Khaki Bill'. The French crowds watching the show may not have guessed, but all the soldiers knew that the 28th Division was headed against the German positions on the northern edge of the city. 'It was one of the most remarkable attack orders ever issued,' Bradley remarked later to his aide. 'I don't think many people realized the men were marching from parade into battle.'

On the Channel coast, the Canadian First Army had to capture the great port of Le Havre, while the Second British Army pushed north-east into the Pas de Calais towards some of the German V-weapon sites. Despite the exhaustion of tank drivers and a terrible storm on the night of 30–31 August, the Guards Armoured Division seized Amiens and the bridges over the Somme with the help of the French Resistance. General der Panzertruppe Heinrich Eberbach, the commander of the Fifth Panzer Army, was taken unawares the next morning. The British advance then managed to drive a wedge between the remains of the Fifth Panzer Army and the Fifteenth Army, which had held the Pas de Calais. The Canadians, led by the Royal Regiment of Canada, the Royal Hamilton Light Infantry and the Essex Scottish, headed for Dieppe where they had suffered so grievously in the disastrous raid two years before.

Allied victory euphoria could not have been greater. The July bomb plot that summer against Hitler had encouraged the idea that disintegration had started, rather like in 1918, but in fact the failure of the assassination attempt had strengthened Nazi domination immeasurably. The G-2 intelligence department at SHAEF blithely claimed, 'The August battles have done it, and the enemy in the west has had it.' In London, the war cabinet believed it would all be over by Christmas, and set 31 December as the end of hostilities for planning purposes. Only Churchill remained wary of the German determination to fight on. In Washington a similar assumption allowed attention to turn increasingly to the still desperate fight against the Japanese in the Pacific. The US War Production Board began cancelling military contracts, including those for artillery shells.

Many Germans also thought the end had come. Oberstleutnant Fritz Fullriede in Utrecht wrote in his diary: 'The West Front is finished, the enemy is already in Belgium and on the German frontier; Romania, Bulgaria, Slovakia and Finland are pleading for peace. It is exactly like 1918.' In a Berlin railway station protesters had dared to put up a banner which read: 'We want peace at any price.' On the eastern front the Red Army had crushed Army Group Centre in Operation Bagration, which had taken them 500 kilometres forward to the gates of Warsaw and the River Vistula. In three months the Wehrmacht had lost 589,425 men on the eastern front and 156,726 in the west.

The dash to the Vistula had encouraged the brave but doomed Warsaw uprising of the Armia Krajowa. Stalin, not wanting an independent Poland, callously allowed the insurgents to be crushed by the Germans. East Prussia, with Hitler's headquarters at the Wolfsschanze near Rastenburg, was also threatened, and German armies were collapsing in the Balkans. Just two days before the liberation of Paris, Romania defected from the Axis as Soviet armies surged across its borders. On 30 August, the Red Army entered Bucharest and occupied the vital oilfields of Ploeşti. The way lay open to the Hungarian plain and the

River Danube stretched ahead into Austria and Germany itself.

In mid-August, General George Patton's Third Army charged from Normandy to the Seine. This coincided with the successful Operation Dragoon landings between Cannes and Toulon on the Mediterranean coast. The threat of being cut off prompted a massive German withdrawal right across the country. Members of the Vichy Milice who knew what awaited them at the hands of the Resistance also set out across hostile territory, in some cases for up to a thousand kilometres, to seek safety in Germany. Improvised 'march groups', a mixture of army, Luftwaffe, Kriegsmarine and non-combatant personnel from the Atlantic coast were ordered to escape east, while attempting to evade the French Resistance along the way. The Wehrmacht began to reinforce a salient around Dijon to receive almost a quarter of a million Germans. Another 51,000 soldiers were left trapped on the Atlantic coast and Mediterranean. Major ports were designated as 'fortresses' by the Führer even though there was no hope of ever relieving them. This denial of reality was described by one German general as being like a Catholic priest on Good Friday who sprinkles his plate of pork with holy water and says: 'You are fish.'

Hitler's paranoia had reached new heights in

the wake of the 20 July bomb plot. In the Wolfsschanze in East Prussia, he went far beyond his earlier jibes that the German general staff was just 'a club of intellectuals'. 'Now I know why all my great plans in Russia had to fail in recent years,' he said. 'It was all treason! But for those traitors, we would have won long ago.' Hitler hated the July plotters, not just because of their treachery, but because of the damage they had done to the impression of German unity, and the effect this had on the Third Reich's allies and neutral states.

At the situation conference on 31 August, Hitler declared: 'There will be moments in which the tension between the Allies will become so great that the break will happen. Coalitions in world history have always been ruined at some point.' The propaganda minister Joseph Goebbels rapidly picked up on the Führer's line of thinking at a conference of ministers in Berlin soon afterwards. 'It is certain that the political conflicts will increase with the apparent approach of an Allied victory, and some day will cause cracks in the house of our enemies which no longer can be repaired.'

The chief of the general staff of the Luftwaffe, General der Flieger Werner Kreipe, noted in his diary on that last day of August: 'In the evening reports arrive of the collapse in the west.' A frenzy of activity continued through most of the night with 'orders, instructions, telephone conversations'. The next morning, Generalfeldmarschall Wilhelm Keitel, the chief of the Oberkommando der Wehrmacht (OKW), asked the Luftwaffe to transfer another 50,000 men to ground forces. On 2 September, Kreipe noted: 'Apparently disintegration has set in in the west, Jodl [chief of the Wehrmacht planning staff] surprisingly calm. The Finns detach themselves.' During that day's conference Hitler began insulting the Finnish leader, Marshal Mannerheim. He also became angry that Reichsmarschall Hermann Göring did not bother to turn up at such a critical moment and even suggested disbanding the Luftwaffe's squadrons and transferring flight crews to flak units.

With Red Army forces now on the East Prussian border, Hitler was afraid of a Soviet parachute operation to capture him. The Wolfsschanze had been turned into a fortress. 'By now a huge apparatus had been constructed,' wrote his secretary Traudl Junge. 'There were barriers and new guard posts everywhere, mines, tangles of barbed wire, watchtowers.'

Hitler wanted an officer whom he could trust to command the troops defending him. Oberst Otto Remer had brought the *Grossdeutschland* guard battalion in Berlin to defeat the plotters on 20 July, so on hearing of Remer's request to be posted back to a field command, Hitler summoned him to form a brigade to guard the Wolfsschanze. Initially based on the Berlin battalion and the *Hermann Göring* Flak-Regiment with eight batteries, Remer's brigade grew and grew. The *Führer Begleit,* or Führer Escort, Brigade was formed in September ready to defend the Wolfsschanze against 'an air landing of two to three airborne divisions'. What Remer himself called this 'unusual array' of combined arms was given absolute priority in weapons, equipment and 'experienced front-line soldiers' mostly from the *Grossdeutschland* Division.

The atmosphere in the Wolfsschanze was profoundly depressed. For some days Hitler retired to his bed and lay there listlessly while his secretaries were 'typing out whole reams of reports of losses' from both eastern and western fronts. Göring meanwhile was sulking on the Hohenzollern hunting estate of Rominten which he had appropriated in East Prussia. After the failure of his Luftwaffe in Normandy, he knew that he had been out-manoeuvred by his rivals at the Führer's court, especially the manipulative Martin Bormann who was eventually to prove his nemesis. His other opponent, Reichs-führer-SS Heinrich Himmler, had been given command of the Ersatzheer — the Replace-ment Army — in whose headquarters the bomb plot had been hatched. And Goebbels appeared to have complete command of the home front, having been appointed Reich Plenipotentiary for the Total War Effort. But Bormann and the Gauleiters could still thwart almost any attempt to exert control over their fiefdoms.

Although most Germans had been shocked by the attempt on Hitler's life, a steep decline in morale soon followed as Soviet forces advanced to the borders of East Prussia. Women above all wanted the war to end and, as the security service of the SS reported, many had lost faith in the Führer. The more perceptive sensed that the war could not end while he remained alive.

Despite, or perhaps because of, the successes of that summer, rivalries were stirring in the highest echelons of the Allied command. Eisenhower, 'a military statesman rather than a warlord' as one observer put it, sought consensus, but to the resentment of Omar Bradley and the angry contempt of George Patton, he seemed bent on appeasing Montgomery and the British. The debate, which was to inflame relations throughout the rest of 1944 and into the new year, had begun on 19 August.

Montgomery had demanded that almost all Allied forces should advance under his command through Belgium and Holland into the

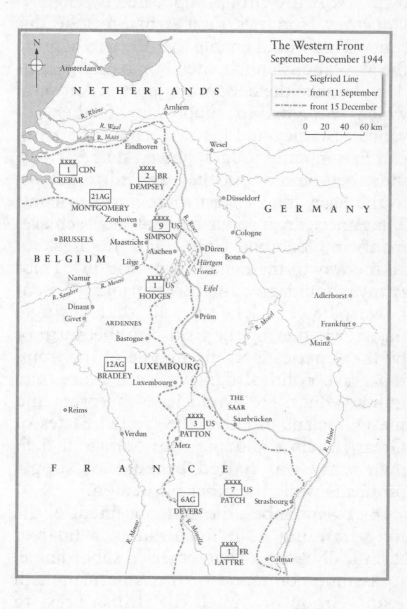

The Western Front
September–December 1944

········· Siegfried Line
– – – – front 11 September
–·–·– front 15 December

0   20   40   60 km

N

Amsterdam

NETHERLANDS

R. Rhine
R. Waal
R. Maas

Arnhem

Eindhoven

Wesel

XXXX
1 CDN
CRERAR

XXXX
2 BR
DEMPSEY

Düsseldorf

21AG
MONTGOMERY

GERMANY

Zonhoven

XXXX
9 US
SIMPSON

R. Roer

Cologne

BRUSSELS

Maastricht

Aachen

Düren
Bonn

BELGIUM

Liège

Hürtgen
Forest

Namur

R. Meuse

XXXX
1 US
HODGES

Eifel

R. Sambre

Dinant

Adlerhorst

Givet

ARDENNES

Prüm

R. Mosel

Frankfurt

Bastogne

Mainz

12AG LUXEMBOURG
BRADLEY

Luxembourg

THE
SAAR

Reims

XXXX
3 US
PATTON

Saarbrücken

Verdun

Metz

R. Rhine

F   R   A   N   C   E

6AG
DEVERS

XXXX
7 US
PATCH

Strasbourg

R. Meuse

R. Moselle

XXXX
1 FR
LATTRE

Colmar

industrial region of the Ruhr. After this proposal had been rejected, he wanted his own 21st Army Group, supported by General Courtney Hodges's First Army, to take this route. This would enable the Allies to capture the V-weapon launch sites bombarding London and take the deep-water port of Antwerp, which was vital to supply any further advances. Bradley and his two army commanders, Patton and Hodges, agreed that Antwerp must be secured, but they wanted to go east to the Saar, the shortest route into Germany. The American generals felt that their achievements in Operation Cobra, and the breakout all the way to the Seine led by Patton's Third Army, should give them the priority. Eisenhower, however, knew well that a single thrust, whether by the British in the north or by the Americans in the middle of the front, ran grave political dangers, even more than military ones. He would have the press and the politicians in either the United States or Great Britain exploding with outrage if their own army was halted because of supply problems while the other pushed on.

On 1 September, the announcement of the long-standing plan for Bradley, who had technically been Montgomery's subordinate, to assume command of the American 12th Army Group prompted the British press to feel aggrieved once again. Fleet Street saw the reorganization as a demotion for Montgomery because, with Eisenhower now based in France, he was no longer ground forces commander. This problem had been foreseen in London, so to calm things down Montgomery was promoted to field marshal (which in theory made him outrank Eisenhower, who had only four stars). Listening to the radio that morning, Patton was sickened when 'Ike said that Monty was the greatest living soldier and is now a Field Marshal.' No mention was made of what others had achieved. And after a meeting at Bradley's headquarters next day, Patton, who had led the charge across France, noted: 'Ike did not thank or congratulate any of us for what we have done.' Two days later his Third Army reached the River Meuse.

In any event, the headlong advance by the US First Army and the British Second Army to Belgium proved to be one of the most rapid in the whole war. It might have been even faster if they had not been delayed in every Belgian village and town by the local population greeting them with rapture. Lieutenant General Brian Horrocks, the commander of XXX Corps, remarked that 'what with champagne, flowers, crowds, and girls perched on the top of wireless trucks, it was difficult to get on with the war'. The Americans also found that their welcome in Belgium was far warmer and more enthusiastic than it had been in France. On 3 September, the Guards Armoured Division entered

Brussels to the wildest scenes of jubilation ever.

The very next day, in a remarkable *coup de main,* Major General 'Pip' Roberts's 11th Armoured Division entered Antwerp. With the assistance of the Belgian Resistance, they seized the port before the Germans could destroy its installations. The 159th Infantry Brigade attacked the German headquarters in the park, and by 20.00 hours the commander of the German garrison had surrendered. His 6,000 men were marched off to be held in empty cages in the zoo, the animals having been eaten by a hungry population. 'The captives sat on the straw,' Martha Gellhorn observed, 'staring through the bars.' The fall of Antwerp shocked Führer headquarters. 'You had barely crossed the Somme,' General der Artillerie Walter Warlimont acknowledged to his Allied interrogators the following year, 'and suddenly one or two of your armoured divisions were at the gates of Antwerp. We had not expected any breakthrough so quickly and nothing was ready. When the news came it was a bitter surprise.'

The American First Army also moved fast to catch the retreating Germans. The reconnaissance battalion of the 2nd Armored Division, advancing well ahead of other troops, identified the enemy's route of withdrawal, then took up ambush positions with light tanks in a village or town just after dark. 'We would let a convoy get within [the] most effective range of our weapons before we opened fire. One light tank was used to tow knocked out vehicles into hiding among buildings in the town to prevent discovery by succeeding elements. This was kept up throughout the night.' One American tank commander calculated that from 18 August to 5 September his tank had done 563 miles 'with practically no maintenance'.

On the Franco-Belgian border, Bradley's forces had an even greater success than the British with a pincer movement meeting near Mons. Motorized units from three panzer divisions managed to break out just before the US 1st Infantry Division sealed the ring. The paratroopers of the 3rd and 6th Fallschirmjäger-Divisions were bitter that once again the Waffen-SS had saved themselves, leaving everybody else behind. The Americans had trapped the remnants of six divisions from Normandy, altogether more than 25,000 men. Until they surrendered they were sitting ducks. The 9th Infantry Division artillery reported: 'We employed our 155mm guns in a direct fire role against enemy troop columns, inflicting heavy casualties and contributing to the taking of 6,100 prisoners including three generals.'

Attacks by the Belgian Resistance in the Mons Pocket triggered the first of many reprisals, with sixty civilians killed and many houses set on fire. Groups of the Armée Secrète from the Mouvement National Belge, the Front de l'Indépendance and the Armée Blanche worked closely with the Americans in the mopping-up stage.* The German military command became angry and fearful of a mass rising as their forces retreated through Belgium to the safety of the Westwall, or Siegfried Line as the Allies called it. Young Belgians flocked to join in the attacks, with terrible consequences both at the time and later in December when the Ardennes offensive brought back German forces, longing for revenge.

On 1 September, in Jemelle, near Rochefort in the northern Ardennes, Maurice Delvenne watched the German withdrawal from Belgium with pleasure. 'The pace of the retreat by German armies accelerates and seems increasingly disorganized,' he wrote in his diary. 'Engineers, infantry, navy, Luftwaffe and artillery are all in the same truck. All of

* The name L'Armée Blanche had nothing to do with the white armies of the Russian Civil War. It had evolved from the secret Belgian intelligence network established under German occupation during the First World War, which was called La Dame Blanche because of the legend that the Hohenzollern dynasty of the Kaiser would fall when the ghost of a white lady appeared.

these men have obviously just been in the combat zone. They are dirty and haggard. Their greatest concern is to know how many kilometres still separate them from their homeland, and naturally we take a spiteful pleasure in exaggerating the distance.'

Two days later SS troops, some with bandaged heads, passed by Jemelle. 'Their looks are hard and they stare at people with hatred.' They were leaving a trail of destruction in their wake, by burning buildings, tearing down telegraph lines and driving stolen sheep and cattle before them. Farmers in the German-speaking eastern cantons of the Ardennes were ordered to move with their families and livestock back behind the Siegfried Line and into the Reich. News of the Allied bombing was enough to discourage them, but most simply did not want to leave their farms, so they hid with their livestock in the woods until the Germans had gone.

On 5 September, the exploits of young *résistants* provoked the retreating Germans into burning thirty-five houses beside the N4 highway from Marche-en-Famenne towards Bastogne, near the village of Bande. Far worse was to follow on Christmas Eve when the Germans returned in the Ardennes offensive. Ordinary people were terrified by the reprisals that followed Resistance attacks. At Buissonville on 6 September the Germans took revenge for an attack two days before.

They set fire to twenty-two houses there and in the next-door village.

Further along the line of retreat, villagers and townsfolk turned out with Belgian, British and American flags to welcome their liberators. Sometimes they had to hide them quickly when yet another fleeing German detachment appeared in their main street. Back in Holland at Utrecht, Oberstleutnant Fritz Fullriede described 'a sad platoon of Dutch National Socialists being evacuated to Germany, to flee the wrath of the native Dutch. Lots of women and children.' These Dutch SS had been fighting at Hechtel over the Belgian border. They had escaped the encirclement by swimming a canal, but 'the wounded officers and men who wanted to give themselves up were for the most part — to the discredit of the British [who apparently stood by] — shot by the Belgians'. Both Dutch and Belgians had much to avenge after four years of occupation.

The German front in Belgium and Holland appeared completely broken. There was panic in the rear with chaotic scenes which prompted the LXXXIX Army Corps to speak in its war diary of 'a picture that is unworthy and disgraceful for the German army'. Feldjäger Streifengruppen, literally punishment groups, seized genuine stragglers and escorted them to a collection centre, or *Sam-*

mellager. They were then sent back into the line under an officer, usually in batches of sixty. Near Liège, around a thousand men were marched to the front by officers with drawn pistols. Those suspected of desertion were court-martialled. If found guilty, they were sentenced either to death or to a Bewährungsbataillon (a so-called probation battalion, but in fact more of a punishment or Strafbataillon). Deserters who confessed, or who had put on civilian clothes, were executed on the spot.

Each Feldjäger wore a red armband with 'OKW Feldjäger' on it and possessed a special identity card with a green diagonal stripe which stated: 'He is entitled to make use of his weapon if disobeyed.' The Feldjäger were heavily indoctrinated. Once a week an officer lectured them on 'the world situation, the impossibility of destroying Germany, on the infallibility of the Führer and on underground factories which should help outwit the enemy'.

Generalfeldmarschall Walter Model's 'Appeal to the Soldiers of the Army of the West' went unheeded when he called on them to hold on, to gain time for the Führer. The most ruthless measures were taken. Generalfeldmarschall Wilhelm Keitel ordered on 2 September that 'malingerers and cowardly shirkers, including officers' should be executed immediately. Model warned that he needed a minimum of ten infantry divisions and five panzer divisions if he were to prevent a breakthrough into northern Germany. No force of that magnitude was available.

The retreat in the north along the Channel coast had been much more orderly, mainly thanks to the delayed pursuit of the Canadians. General der Infanterie Gustav von Zangen had conducted the withdrawal of the Fifteenth Army from the Pas de Calais to northern Belgium in an impressive manner. Allied intelligence was severely mistaken when it stated that 'the only reinforcements known to be arriving in Holland are the demoralized and disorganized remnants of the Fifteenth Army now escaping from Belgium by way of the Dutch islands'.

The sudden seizure of Antwerp may have been a severe blow to the German high command, but over the following days, when the British Second Army failed to secure the north side of the Scheldt estuary, General von Zangen managed to establish defence lines. These included a twenty-kilometre-wide redoubt on the south side of the mouth of the Scheldt called the Breskens pocket, the South Beveland peninsula on the north side and the island of Walcheren. His force soon mustered 82,000 men and deployed some 530 guns which prevented any attempt by the Royal Navy to approach the heavily mined estuary.

Admiral Sir Bertram Ramsay, the Allied naval commander-in-chief, had told SHAEF and Montgomery that the Germans could block the Scheldt estuary with ease. And Admiral Sir Andrew Cunningham, the First Sea Lord, warned that Antwerp would be 'as much use to us as Timbuctoo' unless the approaches were cleared. General Horrocks, the corps commander, later admitted his own responsibility for the failure. 'Napoleon, no doubt, would have realized this,' he wrote, 'but I am afraid Horrocks didn't.' But it was not the fault of Horrocks, nor of Roberts, the commander of the 11th Armoured Division. The mistake lay with Montgomery, who was not interested in the estuary and thought that the Canadians could clear it later.

It was a massive error and led to a very nasty shock later, but in those days of euphoria generals who had served in the First World War convinced themselves that September 1944 was the equivalent of September 1918. 'Newspapers reported a 210-mile advance in six days and indicated that Allied forces were in Holland, Luxembourg, Saarbrücken, Brussels and Antwerp,' wrote the combat historian Forrest Pogue. 'The intelligence estimates all along the lines were marked by an almost hysterical optimism.' The eyes of senior officers were fixed on the Rhine, with the idea that the Allies could leap it in virtually one bound. This vision certainly beguiled Eisenhower, while Montgomery, for his own reasons, had become besotted with it.

2
ANTWERP AND THE GERMAN FRONTIER

At the end of August, just when it seemed as if the German front was on the point of collapse, supply problems threatened to bring Eisenhower's armies to a halt. The French rail network had been largely destroyed by Allied bombing, so around 10,000 tons of fuel, rations and ammunition had to be hauled daily all the way from Normandy in the supply trucks of the US Army's 'Red Ball Express'. The distance from Cherbourg to the front in early September was close to 500 kilometres, which represented a three-day round trip. Liberated Paris alone needed an absolute minimum of 1,500 tons a day.

Only the wealth of American resources could have managed such a task, with some 7,000 trucks racing day and night along one-way routes, consuming almost 300,000 gallons of fuel a day. Altogether some 9,000 trucks were written off in the process. In a desperate attempt to keep up momentum in the dash across France, jerrycans had been delivered to front-line formations by the transport aircraft of IX Troop Carrier Command and even by bombers. But aircraft used up three gallons of aviation fuel for every two gallons of gasoline they delivered. Every aspect of the supply crisis underlined the urgent need to open the port of Antwerp, but Montgomery's focus was on crossing the Rhine.

On 3 September, Montgomery heard that, although a large part of the US First Army would support him in the north, it would not be under his command. Having thought that Eisenhower had agreed to a northern thrust under his sole control, he became exasperated when he heard that Patton's Third Army had not been brought to a halt as he had expected. Montgomery wrote to Field Marshal Sir Alan Brooke, the chief of the imperial general staff, in London on that fifth anniversary of Britain going to war. He revealed his intention to go all out for a Rhine crossing as soon as possible. He evidently felt that was the best way of forcing Eisenhower's hand to give his army group the bulk of the supplies and the command of Hodges's First Army.

Patton, instead of halting his army until the supply situation improved, had secretly stolen a march in his advance towards the Saar. 'In order to attack,' Patton explained in his diary, 'we first have to pretend to reconnoiter and then reinforce the reconnaissance and then finally attack. It is a very sad method of making war.' Patton was quite shameless in getting his own way. Bomber pilots did not grumble when switched to a fuel run, because sometimes when they delivered supplies to Third Army divisions, a case of champagne would be brought to the pilot 'with [the] compliments of General Patton'. Patton could afford to be generous. He had somehow 'liberated' 50,000 cases.

Montgomery was so determined to mount the major strike in the north that he was prepared even to jeopardize the opening of the port of Antwerp for supplies. The new field marshal's operational outline of 3 September revealed that he had dropped the idea of diverting strong forces to clear the Scheldt estuary. This was why Roberts's 11th Armoured Division, on entering Antwerp, had received no orders to advance across the Albert Canal and round into the Beveland peninsula to the northwest where the Germans were starting to prepare positions.

Within the next few days the remnants of the German Fifteenth Army on both sides of the Scheldt started to become a formidable fighting force once more. The German army's extraordinary capacity to recover from disaster had been shown time and time again on the eastern front as well as in the west. Morale was bad, but the determination to

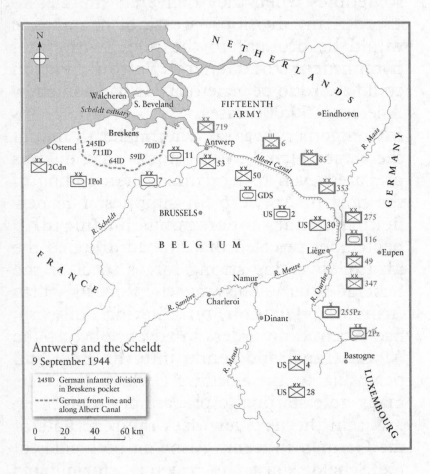

Antwerp and the Scheldt
9 September 1944

245ID German infantry divisions
in Breskens pocket
---- German front line and
along Albert Canal

0   20   40   60 km

fight on had not collapsed entirely. 'Even if all our allies abandon us, we must not lose courage,' an Unteroffizier wrote home. 'Once the Führer has his new weapons deployed, then the Final Victory will follow.'

While Eisenhower recognized the importance of securing the approaches to the port of Antwerp, he too was keen to get a bridgehead across the Rhine. In particular, he wanted to use the newly created First Allied Airborne Army in a major operation. His interest was shared by both General George C. Marshall, the chief of staff in Washington, and the US air force chief General 'Hap' Arnold. The great investment in time and effort building up the airborne arm had spurred on their desire to use it again at the first opportunity.

No fewer than nine plans for its deployment had been considered since the breakout in Normandy, but the speed of the Allied advance meant that every project had been overtaken before it could be launched. The exasperation of the paratroopers waiting on airfields can be imagined, as they repeatedly stood to, with aircraft and gliders packed, and then stood down again. General Patton boasted at a Third Army press conference: 'The damn airborne can't go fast enough to keep up with us.' He then added: 'That is off the record also.'

During the first week of September Field

Marshal Montgomery began to look closely at the possibility of airborne drops to cross the Rhine at Arnhem. Operation Market Garden, to be launched on 17 September, was not merely ambitious. It was shockingly ill planned, with a minimal chance of success, and should never have been attempted. The drop zones, especially in the case of Arnhem, were too far from their bridge objectives to achieve surprise. Plans were not coordinated between the First Allied Airborne Army and the ground forces. The British XXX Corps was expected to charge up a single road for 104 kilometres to relieve the British airborne division at Arnhem, assuming it had secured the bridge there over the Neder Rijn, or lower Rhine. Worst of all, no allowance was made for anything to go wrong, including a change in the weather, which would prevent reinforcements from coming in rapidly.

The American 101st Airborne Division secured Eindhoven, and the 82nd Airborne eventually took Nijmegen and the bridge over the River Waal, only because Generalfeldmarschall Model refused to allow it to be blown up on the grounds that he might need it for a counter-offensive. But determined resistance and constant German flank attacks on the exposed road, soon known as 'Hell's Highway', seriously hampered the advance of the Guards Armoured Division.

Allied intelligence knew that the 9th SS Panzer-Division *Hohenstaufen* and the 10th SS Panzer-Division *Frundsberg* were in the area of Arnhem. But analysts made the fatal mistake of assuming that both formations were so run down after the retreat from France that they would not represent a serious threat. The German reaction to the drop of the British 1st Airborne Division was swift and brutal. Only a single battalion made it to the bridge, and even then it was trapped on the northern side. On 25 September, surviving paratroopers were evacuated across the river. Total Allied losses, British, American and Polish, exceeded 14,000 men. The whole operation did little to enhance American confidence in British leadership.

Allied excitement at the prospect of jumping the Rhine in almost one bound had distracted attention from the more mundane but essential task of securing a proper supply line. Admiral Sir Bertram Ramsay was livid that SHAEF, and especially Montgomery, had ignored his warnings to secure the Scheldt estuary and the approaches to Antwerp. Despite Eisenhower's urging to concentrate on the one major port captured with its dock facilities intact, Montgomery had insisted that the First Canadian Army should proceed with clearing the German garrisons holding out in Boulogne, Calais and Dunkirk. Yet none of these ports, which suffered from demolitions carried out by the defenders, would be navigable for some time.

Eisenhower, largely recovered from a knee injury, at last began to try to clarify Allied strategy. He set up a small advance headquarters near Reims, and on 20 September SHAEF took over the Trianon Palace Hotel at Versailles, an establishment of Belle Epoque grandeur. During the First World War, it had been the headquarters of the Inter-Allied Military Council. On 7 May 1919, Georges Clemenceau had dictated the conditions of the Treaty of Versailles in its main salon, several days before the document was signed in the Hall of Mirrors of the Château de Versailles.

Over the next two weeks, more departments moved into numerous buildings around it, including the huge stables. Soon some 1,800 properties around Versailles were commandeered to house 24,000 officers and men. In Paris, Lieutenant General John C. Lee, the American supply supremo of the Communications Zone, known as 'Com Z', took over 315 hotels and several thousand other buildings and apartments to house his senior officers in style. He also appropriated the Hôtel George V almost entirely for himself. The pompous and megalomaniac Lee even expected wounded soldiers to lie to attention in their hospital beds whenever he appeared on a tour of inspection in boots, spurs and riding whip, accompanied by a fawning staff.

Front-line divisions were outraged that the supply organization should concentrate on its own comforts before anything else, and French authorities complained that American demands were far greater than those of the Germans. One magazine said that SHAEF stood for the 'Societé des Hôteliers Américains en France'. Eisenhower was furious with Lee, who had blatantly contravened his instruction not to colonize Paris, but he never quite summoned up the determination to sack him. Even Patton, who loathed and despised Lee, never dared to cross him in case he retaliated by shutting down supplies to his Third Army.

The Supreme Commander also found that strategic issues had not been clarified, even after the great setback at Arnhem. Once Montgomery had an idea in his head, he could not let go. Ignoring the fact that his own forces had not opened Antwerp to ships and that his pet project of Market Garden had failed, he still argued that the bulk of supplies should be allotted to his army group for a strike into northern Germany. In a letter of 21 September, the day that the British parachute battalion was forced to surrender at Arnhem, Montgomery ticked off his Supreme Commander for not having stopped Patton in his tracks altogether. Significantly, even the Germans thought Montgomery was wrong. General Eberbach, whom the British had captured in Amiens, told fellow generals in Allied captivity: 'The whole point of their main effort is wrong. The traditional gateway is through the Saar.'

Patton argued that Montgomery's plan to lead a 'narrow front' with a 'single knife-like drive toward Berlin' was totally mistaken. Montgomery was far too cautious a commander for such a strategy and his northern route had to cross the main rivers of northern Europe at their widest. Bradley remarked that Montgomery's so-called 'dagger-thrust with the 21st Army Group at the heart of Germany' would probably be a 'butter-knife thrust'. Patton, who was struggling to take the fortified city of Metz, had been told to go over to the defensive, which did not improve his mood. But on 21 September, when Eisenhower referred to Montgomery as 'a clever son of a bitch', Patton was encouraged to believe that the Supreme Commander had at last started to see through the field marshal's manipulative ways. As part of his campaign to be appointed land forces commander, Montgomery had predicted that tight control of the campaign would wane once Eisenhower had assumed command. 'The problem was', as the historian John Buckley emphasized, 'that it was Monty himself as much as anyone, who worked to undermine his chief.'

Eisenhower tried to brush over the differences between Montgomery's proposal and his own strategy of advancing on both the Ruhr and the Saar at the same time. In fact he gave the impression that he supported Monty's single thrust, but just wanted to allow a little flexibility in the centre. This was a grave mistake. He needed to be explicit. Eisenhower knew that he could issue direct orders to Bradley and General Jacob L. Devers, the two American army group commanders, who were his subordinates. But he gave too much leeway to Montgomery because he was an ally and not part of the US Army chain of command. Eisenhower should have known by then that General Marshall in Washington would back him as Supreme Commander, and that Churchill no longer had any influence with President Roosevelt, especially when it came to military decisions. Eisenhower's reluctance to insist that the time for discussion was over and that his orders must be followed enabled Montgomery to keep questioning a strategy with which he disagreed, and chiselling at it constantly to get his own way. Montgomery had no idea of the tensions he was provoking in Anglo-American relations, which would come to a head in December and January.

The situation was not helped by Montgomery's failure to attend an important conference held by Eisenhower on 22 September at his headquarters in Versailles. In his stead, he sent his chief of staff Major General Francis de Guingand, known as 'Freddie', who was liked and trusted by all. American generals suspected that Montgomery did this on purpose so that he could wriggle out of agreements later. The conference focused on the strategy to be adopted as soon as the port of Antwerp was secured. Eisenhower accepted that the main thrust would be made by Montgomery's 21st Army Group, which was to envelop the Ruhr from the north. But at the same time he wanted Bradley's 12th Army Group to cross the Rhine in the region of Cologne and Bonn, to encircle the Ruhr from the south. Eisenhower set all this out in a letter to Montgomery two days later to ensure that there could be no doubt in the field marshal's mind.

Montgomery, having given the task of clearing the approaches to Antwerp to the First Canadian Army, seemed to pay little further attention in that direction. He was more interested in exploiting the Nijmegen salient seized during Operation Market Garden to attack towards the Reichswald, the forest just across the German border. But the Canadians, when they eventually finished in northern France and began the Scheldt operation in early October, found that German resistance was far stronger than imagined. They had a bitter fight on their hands, now that the remnants of the German Fifteenth Army had been given the time to escape and reinforce the island of Walcheren and the South Beveland peninsula.

Eisenhower, prompted by a report from the Royal Navy, was even more concerned at the slow progress. Montgomery became angrily defensive at any implication that he was not doing enough to open Antwerp and argued once more that the US First Army should be placed under his command, to speed the attack on the Ruhr. On 8 October, he again criticized Eisenhower's strategy, but this time to General Marshall himself who was visiting Eindhoven. It was a bad mistake. Even the supremely self-disciplined Marshall nearly lost his temper at this example of what he called Montgomery's 'overwhelming egotism'. The field marshal, devoid of any emotional intelligence, then renewed his onslaught on Eisenhower's command abilities with a paper entitled 'Notes on Command in Western Europe'. Montgomery was almost certainly sharper in his criticisms because of the heavy hints he had heard that his failure to secure the banks of the Scheldt was what had halted the advance of the Allied armies. He even implied that Market Garden had failed because he had not received sufficient support from SHAEF.

Eisenhower replied several days later with a powerful rebuttal which he had shown to

Marshall for his approval. Neither his chief of staff General Walter Bedell Smith nor Marshall would let him soften the draft. Even the rhinoceros-hided Montgomery could not miss the import of one paragraph. 'If you, as the senior commander in this theater of one of the great Allies, feel that my conceptions and directives are such as to endanger the success of operations, it is our duty to refer the matter to higher authority for any action they may choose to take, however drastic.' Montgomery promptly climbed down. 'You will hear *no* more on the subject of command from me. I have given you my views and you have given your answer. That ends the matter . . . Your very devoted and loyal subordinate, Monty.' But for Montgomery, the matter would rumble on for the rest of his days.

The battle for the Scheldt approaches, which finally began on 2 October with a drive north and north-west from Antwerp, was conducted under heavy rain. It took the Canadians, with the support of the British I Corps on their right, two weeks to reach the base of the South Beveland peninsula and the rest of the month to clear it. Another force from II Canadian Corps meanwhile took most of October to clear the large pocket inside the Leopold Canal on the south side of the mouth of the Scheldt. To help take Walcheren, the RAF eventually agreed to bomb the dykes to flood most of the island

and force the German garrison of more than 6,000 men out of their defensive positions. British commando forces from Ostend arrived in landing craft at the western tip and, despite heavy losses, met up with Canadian troops crossing from the captured southern enclave. On 3 November, the last German prisoners were rounded up, making a total of 40,000 Germans captured, but the Canadians and British had suffered 13,000 casualties in the Scheldt operation. Even so, the need to clear the German mines in the estuary meant that the first supply convoy did not enter the harbour of Antwerp until 28 November. That was eighty-five days after the 11th Armoured Division had taken the city by surprise.

The first American patrol crossed on to German soil from north-eastern Luxembourg on the afternoon of 11 September. From high ground, they sighted some concrete bunkers of the Siegfried Line. Many units from then on proclaimed their arrival on Nazi territory by symbolically urinating on the ground. The same day just north-west of Dijon, the French 2nd Armoured Division in Patton's XV Corps, the 2ème Division Blindée, met up with the 1st French Division of the Seventh Army coming up from the south of France. The Allies now had a solid line from the North Sea to Switzerland.

Patton took Nancy on 14 September, but

his Third Army was blocked by the ancient fortifications of Metz and faced hard fighting to get across the Moselle. 'We took enough prisoners', reported an officer, 'to work on the river edge where the Germans were hitting our medics trying to get wounded back in assault boats. They shot and riddled wounded soldiers that could have pulled through. We made the prisoners expose themselves for this work and they even shot them. Finally, we said, "To hell with it," and shot the whole damned bunch.'

German divisions faced different handicaps. A regimental commander with the 17th SS Panzergrenadier-Division *Götz von Berlichingen* complained that his vehicles 'kept breaking down because the petrol was poor. There was water in it. That's the way we are supposed to fight a war! I had absolutely no artillery at all. You know, when our soldiers have to continually haul their own guns around then they soon say: "You can kiss my ass. I'd rather be taken prisoner." ' Such sentiments were certainly not revealed to Führer headquarters. 'Relations between officers and men in the front line remain excellent and give no cause for alarm,' the German First Army reported to the OKW, and on balance that appeared to be true, to judge by letters home.

'The war has reached its climax,' an Obergefreiter wrote to his wife. 'I'm in the sector opposite my birthplace. As a result I can defend my homeland and you with more courage and determination . . . We must never contemplate the unthinkable possibility of defeat.' Others expressed disdain for their enemy. 'He doesn't attack without aircraft and tanks. He's too cowardly for that. He has every imaginable weapon at his disposal.' Another wrote: 'The American infantryman isn't worth a penny. They only operate with heavy weapons and as long as a German machine gun is still firing, the American soldier doesn't advance.' But Obergefreiter Riegler acknowledged that 'Whoever has air superiority is going to win this war, that's the truth.' And Obergefreiter Hoes was bitter about the lack of effect from the V-weapons. 'Why sacrifice more and more men? Allow more and more of our homeland to be destroyed? Why has there been no success with the V-weapons of which so much has been said?'

On 16 September, the day before Market Garden was launched, Hitler astonished his entourage at the Wolfsschanze when he summoned another meeting after the morning situation conference. Generaloberst Alfred Jodl was just speaking of the scarcity of heavy weapons, ammunition and tanks on the western front when, as General der Flieger Kreipe noted in his diary: 'Führer interrupts Jodl. Decision by the Führer, counter-attack

from the Ardennes, objective Antwerp . . .
Our attack group, thirty new Volksgrenadier
divisions and new panzer divisions in addi-
tion to panzer divisions from the east. Attempt to break the boundary between the
British and Americans, a new Dunkirk. Guderian [the army chief of staff responsible for
the Russian front] protests because of the
situation in the East. Jodl points to the
superiority in the air and the expectation of
parachute landings in Holland, Denmark and
northern Germany. Hitler requests 1,500
fighter planes by 1 November! Offensive
should be launched during the bad weather
period, then the enemy cannot fly. Rundstedt
is to take over the command. Preparations up
to 1 November. The Führer again sum-
marizes his decision in a long discourse.
Binds us by obligation to maintain strict
secrecy and asks us to employ few and reli-
able men . . . Briefed Göring who flies back
to Karinhall at night. I am quite tired,
headache.'

Guderian was dismayed by the plan because
he knew that almost as soon as the ground
froze hard enough to carry the Red Army's
T-34 medium tanks, Stalin would launch a
massive offensive against East Prussia and
westward from the Soviet bridgeheads across
the River Vistula. 'OKH [Army High Com-
mand] has serious doubts about the Ardennes
plan,' Kreipe noted.

Hitler, having sacked Generalfeldmarschall Gerd von Rundstedt as commander-in-chief west during the battle for Normandy in July, recalled him in the same role. The 'old Prussian' was seen as the archetypal safe pair of hands. Hitler exploited him as a symbol of rectitude, having corrupted him with money and honours. Although Rundstedt still showed sound military judgement, he remained an alcoholic and had little to do with operational decisions. In December 1941 when Hitler had sacked him for the first time on health grounds, everyone thought that this was a pretence. In fact Rundstedt, exhausted and suffering from a grossly excessive consumption of brandy, had been screaming in his sleep at night, and sometimes had to be held down by his aides and given tranquillizers. That sacking had been sweetened by a 'birthday present' of 400,000 Reichsmarks. More recently, to the disgust of many traditional officers, Rundstedt had presided over Hitler's 'Court of Honour' to expel in disgrace any officer thought to have been connected with the July plot.

Ever since the failed assassination attempt, relations between the Nazi Party and the German army had deteriorated. A captain, whose wife was in Reutlingen east of Strasbourg, recounted: 'The [Nazi Party] Kreisleiter of Reutlingen told a women's meeting that the German army was just a crowd of low-down swine and that if it had not been for the SS and the *Hitler Jugend* Division, the war would have been over long ago. That German officers had slept with French girls and that when the English arrived they had been hauled out of bed, wearing only under-pants, and that he despised every officer. Of course the women cried "Shame!" and my wife left the place amid a general uproar, yet she felt, perhaps naturally enough, not quite so sure of things after that denunciation.' The captain, when he heard of this from his wife, complained to his general. 'That's not the sort of thing to tell the people at home, even if it's partly true, for otherwise they will lose faith in the troops.' But his protest achieved little and must have been reported back. The local Nazis took their revenge against his family by billeting so many people on them that they had no room left to themselves.

Near Aachen, an Obersturmführer Woelky in the 1st SS Panzer-Division *Leibstandarte Adolf Hitler* was taken aback when German women started to object to the likelihood of fighting when they had hoped that the Americans would simply overrun the place. 'We have been lied to and cheated for five years, and promised a golden future, and what have we got?' the most outspoken of them railed. 'I just can't understand how there can be a single German soldier left who will fire another shot.' She was fortunate to have chosen Woelky for her outburst, because he must have been one of the very few in his division to have privately agreed that Germany could not hold out for long. And once the war is over, he thought cynically, 'They will start by re-educating us, the SS, to be democrats.'

3

THE BATTLE FOR AACHEN

On the northern flank of the US First Army the XIX Corps had secured Maastricht, but lacked ammunition and fuel to push on much further. V Corps, on the right flank of the US First Army, had meanwhile advanced into the Belgian and Luxembourg Ardennes. It included the 4th Infantry Division, which Ernest Hemingway had made his own, and the 28th Infantry Division, which had marched through Paris. The glow from that triumphant parade had gone. There seemed little glory in the slow, tedious and often dangerous reduction of the Siegfried Line. 'As we pass a pillbox,' wrote a soldier in the 30th Infantry Division, 'I see a GI sprawled pitifully on the ground, his face in the dirt — helmet on the ground near his head. Bulging from each hip pocket is a never-to-be-eaten K ration.'

Simply to blast a path through the concrete pyramids known as 'dragons' teeth', Sherman tanks needed to fire about fifty rounds. The

Americans found that they first needed to infiltrate the area during the night to get troops in between the German mortar positions and the pillboxes. Assault teams of at least a dozen men, supported by tanks, tank destroyers or anti-tank guns, would take on each pillbox. The concrete was too strong to penetrate except by 155mm self-propelled guns, but tank destroyers firing armour-piercing rounds at the embrasures caused casualties from concussion. 'The wounded come out dazed and bleeding from the nose and mouth,' a US report stated. The Americans also used armour-piercing rounds on the steel doors, or pole or satchel charges containing at least thirty pounds of TNT. 'If they still refuse to surrender, deafen them with a fragmentation grenade down the ventilation shaft,' the same report advised. And a white phosphorus grenade 'placed in the same air-shaft is found to be a great little reviser [of attitudes]'. They should then shout 'Kamerad?' and 'Wir schiessen nicht!' ('We won't shoot!'). 'If all this fails, call a tank to blast the rear of the pillbox or get a tank dozer to fill in the hole [and bury them].'

Soldiers were advised never to enter a pillbox; they should make the defenders come out. 'When the doors and ports had been blown in,' the 41st Armored Infantry Regiment with the 2nd Armored Division reported, 'and enemy automatic weapon fire

81

silenced, the infantry moved to the blind side of the [pill]box and called for the occupants to come out. This was obeyed promptly. At one [pill]box, only 13 prisoners came out. A grenade was thrown through a blasted port and seven more emerged.'

If any German soldier called back to say that they could not move because they were wounded, the advice recommended another explosion. 'After a second charge of TNT, they somehow manage to walk out.' But the attackers should still throw in grenades or use a flamethrower in case anyone was left hiding. Men had to be careful to watch for 'ointment box mines' which were very small, only two inches across and an inch deep. Finally, they needed to seal up the steel doors with blowtorches or a thermite grenade to prevent Germans from reoccupying the pillboxes. One unit had six pillboxes in its sector which had to be retaken three times. On one occasion, a whole platoon, exhausted and wet from the incessant rain, piled into a captured pillbox and fell asleep. A German patrol returned and the whole platoon was taken prisoner without a shot being fired.

In the centre of First Army, VII Corps advanced on the city of Aachen, the ancient capital of Charlemagne and *lieu sacré* of the Holy Roman Empire. The young commander of the corps, Major General J. Lawton Col-